My Friend, JON

ROBERT O. YAGER

ISBN: 978-1-961017-39-9 (sc)
ISBN: 978-1-961017-40-5 (e)

Rev. date: 06/06/2023

Contents

Meeting Jon

Jon was my friend. I am not exactly sure when we first met or talked with one another, but I do remember when I heard about Jon. It was in the summer following our fifth-grade school year when we were both on Little League baseball teams. I played on a team that was sponsored by a service station called Westgate Sohio. Jon played on a team that was sponsored by Spitzer-Rorick Bank. We never played against each other because we were in separate leagues. I heard that Spitzer-Rorick had a pitcher who had a fast ball that was hard to hit. It turned out that that pitcher was Jon. It was a given fact that other teams had pitchers of the same or equal caliber. Our hometown, Toledo, Ohio, produced many great athletes.

On one team, there was a player who we all thought was much older than anyone else because he looked like he shaved. He was right-handed and threw side arm. That was scary. He was nicknamed: "The Old Man." On my team, our pitchers were Billy and Tippy.

In addition, my Dad was our coach. We thought that we were awesome! We won a tournament at the end of the season as did the Spitzer-Rorick Team. Since many of us were in the same grade school class at Christ the King Grade School, it was never determined who had the better team. It would be a heated point of discussion for years to come.

Ironically, Jon and I were in the same first grade class for the school year 1953-1954. The school was Horace Mann, and our teacher was Mrs. Schmidt. I don't remember Jon during that time, but in a photo of that class, there we were. An amazing note is that there were two girls plus me who would graduate from Bowling Green State University in 1969. The next school year, 1954-1955, I went to a brand-new school. Christ the King Elementary School was across the street from Horace Mann. Jon's family had moved so that he was not enrolled in Christ the King. Several years later, his family moved again. Their new residence placed Jon into Christ the King Parish.

Jon and I played on the same CYO (Catholic Youth Organization) basketball team in our 7th and 8th grade years. By this time, the friendship was developing. We were serious about our basketball and had as our favorite team the Ohio State Buckeyes. In that era, the Buckeyes had Jerry Lucas, Mel Nowell, John

Havelicheck, Larry Siegfried, and Bob Knight. Our CYO games were on Saturdays, and we practiced once a week. Since our school did not have a gym, Father Goes (our parish Priest), would rent the public school's gym (Horace Mann) for Wednesday night practice which was conveniently located across the street.

Our fundamentals of dribbling and shooting were very limited. This was reflected by the scores in our games which were relatively low. For example, in one game against Gesu, which was another CYO team, we managed only four points. In another game against Ladyfield, we boosted our total to nine points. Overall, we won eight games, and lost eight games. Jon was the captain of our team, probably because he was the only one who could dribble and shoot. That was 1961.

1953-54 First Grade Horace Mann School, Washington
Local Schools; Bob (Fourth in row 3), Jon (Fourth in row 4).

Our Church School

Our grade school at Christ the King was bursting at the seams. We were the first wave of the post-war Baby Boom. Generally, each class had fifty or more students with one teacher. I remember specifically the number of students in 5th grade. There were fifty-four. Being at the end of the alphabet, I was assigned that number. Jon joined us in the 7th grade. What an asset to our school!

Our daily routine was to go to Mass from 8:15 until 9:15. While some students were having their breakfast (because they went to communion, and you couldn't eat after midnight), we would have our Religion Class. Religion was followed by Math, Geography, and maybe Spelling. An hour was allotted for lunch with some of us having the option of going home. Others brought their lunch and ate at their desks. If you ate fast, you would have more time on the playground. Afternoon instruction consisted of English, History, and an occasional Art class. Science was almost nonexistent.

No foreign language (the Mass was in Latin which was close enough) was offered. Physical Education was what you did on your own during recess.

For our 7th and 8th grade years, our class was moved to the Bingo Hall above the bus garage. There were fifty-four of us under the tutelage of one brave Nun. Overall discipline was good. There was always the threat of having to go to the principal who also taught 5th grade or going to Father Goes to confess your sin. You had to answer to God Almighty. No one wanted those experiences. Besides, your parents would be called.

Once a month, we would all gather in the sanctuary of the church to pray the Rosary. It gave the Nuns and lay teachers a break. During the Rosary and Mass, we had to kneel. Sometimes, the kneelers were not padded. Occasionally, a student would get sick, especially during Mass. Mr. R., our custodian, would immediately arrive on the scene with a bucket of some dry, absorbent stuff to spread over the mess. It would smell like cheese and would permeate the room. Not fun!

It was during these two years that a strong friendship was established between Billy, Oz, Jon and me. All of us lived in the same neighborhood, played on the same basketball team, and would ride our bikes to the Westgate Mall. We began to take an interest in girls.

Jon was the first one to have a girlfriend. Her name was Barbara.

It was toward the end of our 8th grade year that we announced our plans for going to high school. Most of the girls were going to Notre Dame Academy. A few were going to St. Ursula and others to Central Catholic. The boys' plans included either St. Francis or Central Catholic. Then there were those less fortunate (as we were led to believe) that had to go to the public high school. So, it was either Sylvania or Whitmer. Those of us who went to those schools soon found out that there were some very intelligent students enrolled. Jon, Oz and Billy all were accepted to St. Francis.

The summer after eighth grade graduation brought about significant changes to our little group. The biggest event was when Billy announced to us that he and his family were moving to California. Billy's dad was an executive for one of the glass companies in Toledo. He was being transferred to Los Angeles. On Bastille Day, July 14, 1961, a large semi from a moving company pulled up to their home and started the moving process. The four of us held our version of a going away gathering. It would be the last time that the four of us would be together.

It was also during that summer that the students from our class began having boy-girl parties. Jon's mother thought it would be a great idea to have one. The plan was to have the party in their beautifully finished basement on Ariel Drive. Jon, with the input of Oz and me, made up the guest list. Jon also realized that we needed entertainment. His idea was for us to lip-sync a recording of "Blue Moon" by the Marcels. It was a new song going around that not many people had heard. Oz, Jon and I practiced once with Jon deciding that he would sing the lead. I would sing bass, and Oz would fill in. Jon had a brilliant idea that we could pass this off as our own recording. All he had to do was cut out a ring from a dark piece of paper and glue it on the 45rpm to cover the label. No one would know. It would be our own hit single.

The party was scheduled, the guests arrived, and the opportunity presented itself. The three of us took our positions. Jon started the record. Three minutes later we were taking our bows. The applause from our guests was heartwarming. We thought that we were the latest craze in Rock and Roll. However, little George, who was one of the guests, was not convinced. He inquired and wanted to see the record. After examining the 45rpm disk, he announced that the original label had been covered up. Our spoof was over. Foiled again!

1959 Little League Baseball Team, Westgate Sohio. Tippy (Fifth in row one). Billy (Third in row two); Bob (First in row three); Coach Mr. Yager (First in row four).

1961 Eight Grade Basketball Team, Christ the King. Jon (First row with basketball); Oz (Second in row two); Bob (Third in row two); Billy (Fifth in row two)

1961 Eight Grade Graduation, Christ the King. Jon (First in row 4); Billy (Fifth in row); Bob (Seventh in row 4); Oz (Twelfth in row 4).

High School

Jon's parents were having a great deal of success in the home building business. Mr. Wozniak would perform the basic construction, while Mrs. Wozniak would add the finishing touches to the home's décor. One afternoon, Jon called and told me that his parents had undertaken a new project. They had purchased a lot on a lake in Michigan and planned to build a cottage on it. When Jon told me that the lake was Wamplers, I was excited. This was the lake on which my Grandparents had owned a cottage since the late 1920's. Jon's cottage would be built on a beautiful site on a hill overlooking the lake. Jon told me that his parents spent ten thousand dollars for the property. That was an amazing amount of money at the time.

As the summer continued, we were busy playing baseball, cutting grass, and making visits to Wamplers Lake. In August, we realized that that the three of us were not going to be students together anymore. Oz and Jon were headed to St. Francis. They would start their experience as members of the freshmen football team. I was headed to Washington Junior High School. I began my freshman year as a member of the marching band. I would be initiated into this program with a week in August at band camp. I had never been away from home to stay at any camp. To complicate the situation, I only knew one person there. This was going to last one week! I survived. At the end, I admitted that it was an enjoyable experience and accomplishment.

When school started, my mind was far from the seriousness of academics. I was thirteen years old and realized that I would have to shave periodically! My best friends were going to a "real high school," while I was going to a junior high. Jon and Oz talked about their classes, and how they were in lanes assigned according to their entrance test results. I felt overwhelmed with how to open my locker, change classes, and meet new people. There wasn't anyone with whom I felt comfortable. I missed my friends.

It was during our freshman year that Jon and Oz convinced me that I should play football. They enjoyed it. With their encouragement, I made the decision to play during my sophomore year. That decision changed the compass of my life.

In the spring of 1962, I was happy that I had "graduated" from junior high. Finally, I would be in high school, just like my friends. My sophomore year, I tried out for the reserve football team. It was a whole new experience. Getting fit with equipment and trying to find a position where I could just "fit in" was my challenge. I envisioned myself as an end. Nevertheless, our coach, Coach Z., saw my potential as a defensive tackle. I was pleased when at first, I was on the second team. There were other players that had more experience than I did. The coaches soon recognized that the greatest asset I had was that I was "coachable."

By the time our first game came around, I was on the first team as a right defensive tackle! Ironically, our first game was against St. Francis! I don't remember much about the game except that I tackled Oz on one play. The game ended in a tie with neither team scoring: 0 – 0!

Later that season, a tragic event happened that would change the dynamics of our friendship. It was Halloween night, Wednesday, October 31, 1962. The Catholic students who attended a public high school, meaning me, were required to attend CCD (Catechism) classes. These classes were frustrating. I felt that my time would be better spent on doing my Math or English homework. Besides, I was at a time in my life when I was questioning authority and my religion. It was my first experience of rebellion. I skipped out on class. Instead of walking to church, I walked to Oz's home. I found the lights on, but the house was empty. With no direction and time to kill, I wandered the neighborhood. There were kids going house to house in the annual routine of "trick or treat."

When I finally went home, my dad said that two phone calls were for me. One was from the church inquiring where I was. My response was that I had arrived late. I had been outside talking with some friends. The other call was from Jon, and he said that it was urgent that I return his call. When I called, the message was disturbing.

Jon said that Oz collapsed during calisthenics at the start of football practice that day. He was taken by ambulance to the hospital. His condition was uncertain. Two days later, Jon called and informed me that Oz had died. The doctor said that he suffered a brain hemorrhage due to a congenital abnormality in a blood vessel. I was in shock.

The funeral Mass was held at Christ the King Church on Monday November 2, 1962, with Father Goes officiating. Oz's parents asked me to be a pall bearer, along with Jon, Oz's cousin and three members of our eighth-grade class. The entire sophomore class from St. Francis attended the Mass. Oz was buried in Calvary Cemetary. This was my first experience of learning about and dealing with the death of a friend. Only ten months prior, my Grandpa died when he was eighty-five years old. I learned that grief was real and hard.

Years later, when I was researching my family's genealogy, I was in Calvary Cemetary. I inquired about the location of Oz's grave. I was informed at the cemetery office that there was no marker to identify his grave. I said a prayer at the section where his remains lay. I realized once again that I had lost a truly great friend. Of the four of us, now only Jon and I were together.

The remainder of 1962 and during the winter of 1963, Jon and I had one memorable event. That occurred when Whitmer played St. Francis in basketball. Jon and I were both on our school's reserve teams. Jon played in the game, while I kept my bench seat warmed. St. Francis won both the reserve and varsity games. We both wished Oz were there.

That spring I played on Whitmer's reserve baseball team. It was another experience of sitting on the bench. A realization occurred to me that my baseball playing days were over. Jon wasn't playing baseball. "Times, they were a changin!"

That summer, we both had our own agendas. Jon was working with his dad, while I had lawns to mow. Occasionally, Jon would invite me to spend a weekend at Wamplers Lake. One Saturday night around ten o'clock, I remember standing on the dock by the lake and being amazed at the multitude of stars that were visible. As I was gazing upward, I happened to see one very faint point of light that was moving slowly. It was a satellite. Could it have been Sputnik? We also both learned to drive Jon's speed boat and water ski. Skiing wasn't easy at first, but once we were on top of the water, we were euphoric.

Our junior year began with the challenge of trying to be part of our respective varsity football teams. Whitmer and St. Francis had really good players in the senior class ahead of us. Being in the starting lineup was going to be difficult if not impossible. Jon and I were trying very hard to make an impact. The goal for both of us was to earn a varsity letter.

One Saturday in September, the coaches at Whitmer took advantage of an offer by the University of Michigan for high school players to attend one of their home games. The day was sunny and after our Saturday film session, we loaded into cars and headed to Ann Arbor. This was my first opportunity to be on the campus of a big university. It was impressive. Michigan's opponent that day was Navy with Roger Staubach as their quarterback. The stadium had many empty seats, but the atmosphere was electric.

When I returned home, Jon called and invited me to spend Saturday night with him and his parents at Wamplers Lake. It was that evening while standing at the shore of the lake and remembering the experience of the day, that I decided that I wanted to go to college. My life and academic world had a focal point.

Jon's older brother was on a full football scholarship at the University of Toledo. He was a starter on both offense and defense. The rules at that time were such that players had to play both ways. That rule was quickly changed the next year, and in turn, allowed more athletes to play the game. On a Saturday in October, Jon called to find out if I was interested in going to a game at the University of Toledo. An hour before kickoff, a car pulled into my driveway. Mr. Wozniak had just purchased a new blue Pontiac Bonneville convertible. The top was down, and in the front seat with Mr. Wozniak at the wheel were Mrs. Wozniak and her sister. Jon and I occupied the back seat. It was my first ride in a convertible. I was amazed at the open-air view.

Jon's older brother had a rocky relationship with his parents at that time. From what little knowledge of the situation that I had; the problem centered around a girl whom his parents did not approve of. At the time of that football game, he had found a new girl that met his parents' approval. As a reward, Mrs. Wozniak gave him a brand-new sweater that cost fifty dollars. That romance didn't stand the test of time, but the sweater certainly did!

As our football seasons came to an end, we both managed to acquire enough playing time to earn varsity letters. Jon proceeded to make the varsity basketball team while I was on Whitmer's "C" basketball team. It would be my last experience on a basketball team that had a coach. The next winter I played on a CYO team. On that team we did not have a coach. We had to figure things out on our own.

In June, prior to our senior year, we had an opportunity to earn some money. Jon had found out through his brother that the assistant football coaches at the university had a program (more like a scheme) in which high school boys could sell aluminum door-cleaner to the folks of Toledo. I am not certain as to how we obtained our bottles of cleaner. Did we pay in advance for them and then be reimbursed later? Nevertheless, Jon was our sales manager. The main reason Jon was the leader was that he had a car. It was a blue 1955 Ford station wagon.

Our team of four eager young men was assigned to a neighborhood to work. Jon would drive until a house with an aluminum door was spotted. Then one of us with plastic pail, brush and a bottle of the special cleaner in hand would bolt from the car with the goal of making a sale. When the homeowner answered the doorbell, we would begin our sales pitch. We guaranteed our product would work and asked permission to demonstrate the product on the homeowner's storm door. If the owner agreed, we would brush the cleaner onto a small corner on the outside of the door. It really did brighten up the aluminum! Then the homeowner was faced with a significant decision. Buy the product for five dollars a bottle, and finish the project or, decline the offer and let a bright shiny square be forever present on the outside corner of the door. Of the five dollars charged, we got to keep a dollar and fifty cents. We had the job for two weeks. By that time, our crew had covered our assigned section of the city. It was my first experience with door-to-door sales. I was convinced that it wasn't a very good career choice.

The time had arrived. It was the summer before our long-awaited senior year. Football began in a few weeks, and we wanted to be prepared. Jon's brother was introduced to lifting weights at the university. In the garage at their home, he had set up several weightlifting stations. We could do the bench press, squats, and pull downs. Our thinking was that we would be far ahead of our teammates who knew nothing about lifting weights. We didn't know much either, but we learned about sets and reps. It was a great opportunity.

Jon turned seventeen that spring. I would not turn seventeen until December. I played my senior season of football at the age of sixteen. Both of our seasons were moderately successful. Whitmer's record was 4-5-1. Both St. Francis and Whitmer lost to the city champ, Macomber. Macomber's best player that year was Rufus Mayes who would go on to play for Ohio State and the Cincinnati Bengals.

Our senior football seasons had one significant contrast. Whitmer's home games were played on Friday nights under the lights. Jon's team in the City League had to play their games on Saturday mornings or afternoons. Because of riots prior and during games of the previous year, the league's leaders and school principals decided to let the games continue but have them played in the daylight hours.

By game nine, there was a dramatic realization that the 1964 senior season would soon be over. We had worked so hard and been so excited. It lasted ten games. It was a lesson in life as to how fleeting time is.

On December 6th of 1964, I turned seventeen. Jon was playing varsity basketball. I had an opportunity to earn some money. After school for a couple of hours and eight hours on Saturday, I worked as a custodian at Christ the King Church and School. I earned a dollar twenty-five an hour and began paying into the Social-Security system. I earnestly saved my money in our Church's Credit Union.

That winter a photograph appeared in the Toledo newspaper. It showed Jon and his older brother posed in front of the Nike Missile and the football stadium at the University of Toledo. The missile was aimed at Toledo's archrival: Bowling Green State University. In the article under the photograph, it said that Jon had signed his letter of intent to attend and play football for the Toledo Rockets.

As a reward for his commitment to the University, Jon's parents bought him a new Mustang that was gold with a black convertible top. With that car, Jon had to manage a standard transmission. His only complaint was that the car only had a six-cylinder engine. He said that his mother didn't trust him with a Mustang that would have a V-8. Later that summer while driving home, Jon was trying to make a turn from Harvest Lane onto Ariel Drive. Unfortunately, he was rear-ended. I remember that night after the accident because Jon walked the three blocks to our home. Shaken, he knocked on the door and asked if he could use our phone to call his parents. The car was later considered by the insurance company to be a total loss. The replacement would be a blue Mustang convertible. It was amazing that Jon had walked away from the accident with no injuries.

As for my future in football at the college level, I was contacted by two colleges. I made a visit to Defiance College but found that their facilities, both academic and athletic, to be very limited. My Dad said that the high school library at Whitmer had more books than the college library, and the biology lab was very ill equipped, almost out of date. My second visit was to Kent State University. There I was offered the opportunity to be a walk-on player. After visiting with several of their players, I determined that I was too small and too slow to play at that level. My decision was that I would be a serious academic student. I enrolled at Bowling Green State University.

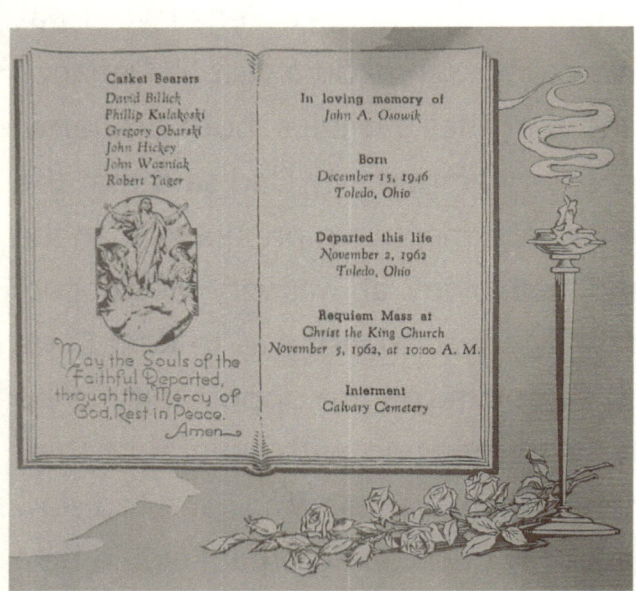

Casket Bearers

David Billick
Phillip Kulakoski
Gregory Obarski
John Hickey
John Wozniak
Robert Yager

May the Souls of the
Faithful Departed,
through the Mercy of
God, Rest in Peace.
Amen

In loving memory of
John A. Osowik

Born
December 15, 1946
Toledo, Ohio

Departed this life
November 2, 1962
Toledo, Ohio

Requiem Mass at
Christ the King Church
November 5, 1962, at 10:00 A. M.

Interment
Calvary Cemetery

John Osowik

John Osowik, 15, of 4542 Haddington Dr., died today in St. Vincent's Hospital, where he was admitted Wednesday after suffering a brain hemorrhage.

A sophomore at St. Francis de Sales High School and a member of the reserve football team, young Osowik complained Wednesday of a headache while taking calesthentics. Dr. Theron Hopple said earlier that the boy suffered a "brain hemorrhage due to a congenital abnormality in the blood vessel."

Among survivors are his parents, Mr. and Mrs. Alex Osowik.

The body will be in the Welsh-Hood Mortuary.

John Osowik

Services for John A. Osowik, 15, of 4542 Haddington Dr., who died yesterday in St. Vincent's Hospital, will be Monday at 10 a.m. in Christ the King Church. Burial will be in Calvary Cemetery. The body will be in the Foth Mortuary, Sylvania Avenue, after 2 p.m. today.

A lifelong Toledo resident, young Osowik was a sophomore at St. Francis High School and a member of its reserve football team. He was a member of Christ the King Church and the Catholic Youth Organization.

Surviving are his parents, Mr. and Mrs. Alex Osowik, brothers, Dennis and Thomas, and grandparents, Mr. and Mrs. Louis Billick, all of Toledo.

The Rosary will be recited tomorrow at 7:30 p.m. by St. Francis students, and also at ...

John Osowik

The honour which you conferred
upon our loved one
by acting as casket bearer
is gratefully acknowledged
and deeply appreciated

The Osowik Family

Remebering Oz

Another Wozniak Joins TU Grid Forces

Bob Wozniak, right, former University of Toledo lineman,
points out some of the TU campus landmarks to younger
brother, Jon. The younger Wozniak, captain of St. Francis
DiSales' football team last season, signed a football grant
in aid at TU. The Rockets are in the final week of spring
practice, which close with the second annual Varsity-
Old-Timers game Saturday at the Glass Bowl at 8 p.m.

Jon and his brother Bob in a photo that appeared in a
Toledo newspaper, circa 1965

College

As the summer went by, we would get together only on occasion. We were both working to have some spending money. Jon again worked for his dad, while I found new employment. My Uncle Moe who worked for the city, told my dad and me that the city was hiring for the city's weed mowing crews. I interviewed, provided a valid driver's license, and was hired. I made two dollars an hour. The mowing crews worked ten-hour days and eight hours on Saturday. My first check was close to two-hundred dollars. By getting a six cent an hour raise every year, I stayed for five summers. What an opportunity to always have a summer job between my four years of college! The last three years, I was made a supervisor. Being a supervisor required that I had to use my green 1960 Volkswagen to carry all tools and maps that were needed. In addition, I was given a voucher for one-hundred gallons of gas per month. Wow!

Because I was working fifty-eight hours per week, Jon and I would get together only occasionally. Sometimes I would be invited to go to Wamplers Lake. Other times we would just drive around the city. One favorite event was to "cruise the hut." The White Hut had two locations in west Toledo, and it was a favorite hangout for young people. One evening however, we cruised by The Centennial Terrace. The marquee at the entrance listed a musical group called "The Byrds." Their leader was Roger McGuinn, and they featured David Crosby. The group had just released the song: "Mr. Tambourine Man." It was a very sparse audience made up mostly of local hippie types. We were obviously not part of the "in-crowd" that night, but their music was unique. Little did we know...

In 1968, we completed our junior year of college. In June of 1969 we both graduated and received our Bachelor's Degrees. In that summer of 1969, Jon became engaged. They were to be married that fall. Jon asked me to be the best man in their wedding.

Teaching Careers

I was in my first year of teaching after having graduated from Bowling Green State University. I had signed a contract to teach Biology and Anatomy/Physiology at Memorial High School in St. Marys, Ohio. In addition, I contracted to coach the Freshman basketball team. My salary for that year was $6,200. The first payroll check that I received was less than the payroll check that I had received from the City of Toledo for mowing weeds. I was devastated.

Jon was in his first year of teaching Social Studies at his alma mater, St. Francis. Jon was an assistant on the football staff, plus being the freshmen basketball coach. At the conclusion of our basketball coaching seasons, the coaches could attend the finals of the state tournament. The finals were held in St. John Arena on the campus of Ohio State University. Much to my surprise, once I had settled in to watch the first game, Jon came walking up the steps in the arena. His seat was adjacent to mine. The OHSAA had issued tickets alphabetically by school name. That was an amazing coincidence.

In 1970, I began taking graduate classes at the University of St. Francis in Fort Wayne, Indiana. It was there that I met Ann Gallatin. We were married on August 14, 1971. Jon was my best man. Mr. and Mrs. Wozniak, Jon's parents, along with Jon's aunt, were in attendance. It was moving how our friendship had deepened.

That fall, I began my teaching career at Heritage High School, Monroeville, Indiana. I stayed there for thirty-six years. In those years, Jon and I would get together at least once a summer. We would meet at Wamplers Lake, or I remember driving to Alpena, Michigan where Jon and his wife lived, along with their young son. Jon's wife had procured a position in special education, and Jon had a teaching job. Later, she had a promotion with the school district in East Lansing, Michigan. They established their residence in Okemos, Michigan. When we would get together, we sometimes would go fishing, or we would sit around and tell stories of the "good ole days."

When their son graduated from high school, Jon sent us an invitation to a party given in his honor. Ann and I accepted and had a great time. It was wonderful seeing Mr. and Mrs. Wozniak, although Mrs. Wozniak was having difficulty with arthritis. At the gathering, Jon invited me to come up to their place in the summer, as his son was chosen to play in the East-West Football All Star game. That summer I traveled to Jon's place. His parents were there. The four of us went to the game in Mr. Wozniak's station wagon. Jon's parents were in the front, while Jon and I sat in the back. Once underway, I asked Jon about his brother. Jon responded: "You didn't hear about that? I will tell you later." Meanwhile, the game was played in the stadium of Michigan State and his son played well. It would be his last football game since he didn't pursue the sport further. Later that evening Jon told me the story of his brother.

His brother was married and had a daughter for whom he had purchased a car that had a large horsepower output. She was killed in an accident involving that car. Being distraught, he went to his parents, borrowed his dad's rifle, went to his parents' gravesite and took his life. That was a shocking and sad revelation.

The visits that Jon and I had together became fewer and fewer. He and his wife came to my daughter's graduation from high school. When Mrs. Wozniak passed away, I drove to Toledo to be at her Wake. After the Mass, there was a gathering at Gesu Church. Jon's family celebrated her life with relatives and friends. At the luncheon, I noticed that the relationship between

Jon and his wife seemed strained. What was going on, I wasn't certain. Eventually, sadly, they were divorced.

In the summer of 1998, prior to the start of our football season, I decided to go to Wamplers Lake and visit Jon. He wasn't at the lake cottage, but upon inquiry at the local party store/bait shop, I found that Jon had moved into a townhome on Wamplers Lake. When I knocked on the door, a surprised Jon answered the door. Now, I am the type of person who likes to call ahead before I arrive unannounced, but Jon's phone number was continuously changing. He told me that he would drop the phone in the lake or somehow lose it, requiring a new one with a different number. Jon's place was a wreck. A table was broken in the living room. Jon seemed so very distant. We talked about football, and football recruiting. Nothing was ever discussed about the divorce, but I knew Jon was not himself.

I had an opportunity to invite Jon to one of our games. He didn't come that year, but he did come to a game a few years later. We were playing at Angola High School. Jon came to the game and sat in the first row. After the game, we visited for a while. Jon was impressed with the size of our players. He even commented that we had some "real men" playing. I was thrilled to see Jon, but disappointed that we lost the game.

In October of 2012, I happened to read in the Toledo Blade that Jon's dad passed away. I did not receive a phone call about his death. I just happened to read The Blade's obituaries that day. I made the trip to Toledo and spent a couple of hours with Jon, his son, and Jons' new wife. Jon said that the final years of Mr. Wozniak's life were hard. He was living in assisted living and grew weaker every day. Jon was living both in Florida and in Michigan. His wife was teaching in Florida. She and Jon would spend the winters there. In the spring, Jon would go back to Michigan where he was an assistant track coach. His area was coaching shot put and discus throwers, both male and female at Okemos High School. He said that he had a lot of success with many throwers making it to the state finals. Jon said that while he was in Florida, his dad would call. Jon would catch a flight to Detroit, take care of what his dad needed, then fly back to Florida.

I told Jon that Ann and I wanted him to attend our 40th anniversary party. My daughters sent him an invitation, and then tried to call. Both attempts were unsuccessful. Jon finally answered. He said that the cottage where he had been living at Wamplers Lake had caught fire and burned to the ground. What happened was that he was going to watch a football game one Saturday afternoon and went to the nearest

Quick Mart/Bait Store. When he returned, the place was ablaze. Fortunately, no one was hurt. He said that he sold the property to a neighbor. The money would go to pay off some of the nursing home bills that his dad had incurred. It was the last time that Jon and I would be together.

The wedding of Robert O. Yager and Ann E. Gallatin, held on August 14, 1971. Jon is the best man.

Jon and Bob checking the time before the wedding ceremony.

Jon keeping from a potential escape before the wedding.

A gathering of friends of the groom following the wedding.

Tragic News

Five years later, in the summer of 2017, my wife, Ann, died on June 12th. Following Ann's passing, I sent a text to Jon telling him of this bad news, but I did not receive a response. A few days later, I called his son's law office in Tampa. The secretary took my message that I was inquiring about Jon. I did not receive a call back. On July 22, I decided to pursue this situation a bit further. I visited Jon's wife's Facebook page. After scrolling down through several items, I came to an item that said that there would be a memorial for Jon! I know what memorials mean. It was a rainy Saturday in mid-July that would be one of the saddest days of my life. I had lost my wife, and now my best friend.

I sent a text to his wife, and she responded. She said that she had been looking for my information. She said that she remembered me. She further explained: Jon died February 23, 2017, while we were in Florida. He was coming down with a cold and had not felt well for a couple of days. The situation became serious, so

I called 911. He died about twenty minutes after the emergency people got there. He was in his room. The emergency people laid him down to attach his heart to the EKG machine, and they lost him very suddenly. They tried for about an hour to revive him, but he was gone. We were all in shock. I thought of you but could not find you. I had him cremated and brought him back to Toledo, where he is buried with his family. Both Jon's son and I were in shock! She told me that she had been going through his photos to send them to his son. She also said that if you would like to call his son, he was in Tampa, Florida, where he has a law office. She also provided his office email address. In a later text from her, she said that: "He loved you like a brother." This comment meant so much to me.

After reading this message, I remembered the date on which Jon passed. It was on Ann's birthday, February 23, 2017, that my friend Jon died.

In a later exchange of text messages with Jon's first wife, she said: "Jon had been having some health issues but nothing debilitating. He died of a sudden heart attack and was dead on arrival at the hospital. The memorial was held in Okemos in May when his second wife went back to Michigan." She went on to say that it was a shock for his son. He and Jon were going to the Tiger's game that next day in Lakeland, Florida. His son was mourning that he never got to say "Goodbye."

When I was doing genealogical research on my family, I hit a dead end on my family research. Out of curiosity, I put Jon's last name, Wozniak, into the quest. I came up with Jon's cause of death. It was identified as influenza. Therefore, it is not completely clear how he died.

Because of his loyalty to the track athletes at Okemos High School, and their success, Jon was posthumously named to the Okemos Hall of Fame in 2017. He was also named as a finalist to the National High School Athletic Coaches Association Coach of the Year. What a great man!

Congratulations, my friend, on a job well done! Someday, we will get to go on that fishing trip and catch up on our stories. There is still that record bass that needs to be caught.

With loving memories,
Your Friend,
Bob

www.ingramcontent.com/pod-product-compliance
Lightning Source LLC
Chambersburg PA
CBHW031239120626
46545CB00003B/1194